Dedication ...

I dedicate this book to:
My husband Merlin
& our puppy Tico,
My brother Tommy
My children:
David, Holly, Julie, Brian & Elijah
My grandchildren:
Hayley & Xan
My Parents: Dorothy & Eric
And in loving memory of my Dad
Gustave Raymond Anderson

Sweet Pink

甜嘴粉红

By Joan Schaefer

Allow me to introduce ...

This Sweet Pink Production
Book Belongs to:

··

Tommy was in the pilot seat above the black clouds ... with great flying skill he eased the silver jet out of the tornado zone undamaged.

"It's time to get up," Mom called rather loudly! "You're going to Grandfather's house today!"

Tommy's eyes popped open and the dream slipped away.

"Yippee," he shouted as he jumped into his shorts.

At the top of the stairs Tommy grabbed the banister with both hands, stretched his foot up, over and W-H-O-O-S-H he landed at the bottom.

"Eee Gads!" Mom gasped ...

"I was careful," said Tommy as he sat down at the kitchen table and ate hot buttered toast. It was a lovely day, he realized as he saw the sun shining in the window.

"Sandwiches and apples are in your backpack," Mom said, "I also put a treat in for Grandfather's parrot."

汤米坐在飞机师的位置上，他的飞机正在乌云上飞行......他熟练地驾驶着银色的喷射机，轻易的穿过龙卷风区域而丝毫无损。

"该起床了"，妈妈大声喊他。"你今天去爷爷的家！"

汤米睡梦惺忪中听见妈妈说去爷爷的家，眼睛马上睁大："啊，好极了！"。他兴奋地从床上大叫着跳入他的牛仔裤。

汤米以手抓住楼梯的栏杆，向上缩起他的脚，飞快地从上面滑到地下。

"哎呀，你又滑楼梯了！"妈妈担心地说。

"我很小心的。"汤米边说边坐在厨房的桌旁吃着热腾腾的奶油松饼。

"I don't want a treat for that bird," Tommy wailed. "It always screeches at me."

"That parrot is Grandfather's special friend," Mom scolded, "you be nice to her."

Out in the hall Tommy put his backpack on and pulled the buckle tight.

"Don't talk to any strangers," Mom warned.

"I won't," Tommy called as he left.

The elevator dropped swiftly to the street floor. Pigeons scattered as Tommy happily jogged along the concrete walks. Flapping his arms he imitated the steady strokes of the pigeon's flight.

"I wish I could fly too," he murmured.

这是晴朗的一天，灿烂的阳光在窗边闪耀着。

"三明治和苹果都放在你的背包里，" 妈妈说： "我也放了一些食物给爷爷的鹦鹉吃。"

"我不想请那只鸟吃，" 汤米嘟着嘴说。"它总是对着我发出恐惧的叫声。"

"那只鹦鹉是爷爷一个特别的朋友，" 妈妈轻责他， "你该好好的对它。" 汤米在大厅里背上了背包，

小心的扣上扣子， 准备出发到爷爷家去。 "不要跟任何陌生人说话，" 妈妈提醒汤米。
"我不会。" 汤米边说边走。

电梯很快地到了地面，汤米沿着街道一蹦一跳地跑着。 汤米摆动胳膊模仿鸽子飞行的动作，

汤米的脚步声驱散了鸽子群。 "希望有一天我能飞行"。 他低声地说。

Out of breath Tommy slowed to a walk when he reached the waterfront. His head filled with all the smells of the sea. Grandfather's house was at the 59th street pier. Halfway down the dock Tommy disappeared into Grandfather's houseboat. Only Sweet Pink, Grandfather's parrot, was inside. In the kitchen he found chocolate bars on the counter, so Tommy ate them. Sweet Pink began to screech furiously, "BRAT! BRAT! BRAT!" She was pointing her wing right at him.

Tommy wished he could hide, then, he heard Grandfather's heavy steps closing in. The door opened. Grandfather gently lifted him from behind the door. Tommy's mouth was a huge circle of chocolate and all of Grandfather's chocolate bars were gone.

Weepy and full Tommy sobbed, "I'm sorry."

Grandfather held him close and whispered, "That's OK, but next time you ask me first."

Tommy smiled and nodded.

跑着跑着，汤米喘着气减慢了速度，慢慢地走到了海边。他的头发吸满了海水的咸味。
爷爷的房子就在码头区的第59街上。在码头区走了一段路，
就到了爷爷居住的平地船屋。爷爷不在家，只有甜嘴粉红在 — 它是爷爷的鹦鹉。
在厨房里他发现有一块巧克力在桌上，汤米拿起来吃了。甜嘴粉红愤怒地大叫

"小贼！小贼！小贼！小贼！"并且用翅膀指向汤米。
汤米真希望他能藏起来，然后他听见爷爷重重的脚步声渐渐地近了。门打开了。

爷爷轻轻地把他从门后面抱起。汤米满嘴是巧克力，他吃光了爷爷的巧克力。

汤米泪汪汪的呜咽着，"对不起。"爷爷在他耳边轻声地说"没关系，

但下次你要跟爷爷先说一声。"汤米微笑着点头。

Grandfather put him down. "I'll be back shortly, I have to get my paper," he said.

"What should I do?" Tommy asked.

"Do me a favor and make friends with Sweet Pink," Grandfather suggested.

"I'll try," Tommy promised.

Grandfather left.

Tommy turned toward the bird. "OK, tattletale parrot, how can we ever be friends?"

To Tommy's surprise Sweet Pink opened her hinged beak wide. "For a starter, you should have respect and call me by my name!"

Stunned at Sweet Pink's speech, Tommy spoke up. "OK, but don't call me a brat anymore!"

"We've got a deal," Sweet Pink cawed.

爷爷把他放下。 "我很快就回来, 我得去拿我的文件，" 他说。

"那我干什么好?" 汤米问爷爷。"跟甜嘴粉红交个朋友," 爷爷建议。"我试试看，"

汤米答应。 爷爷走了。

汤米转向了鹦鹉。"好, 搬弄是非的鹦鹉,我们怎么能成为朋友?"

汤米看着甜嘴粉红张开了像被铰链接合的嘴说： "既然你希望我们成为朋友,

你 尊敬我，叫我的名字!" 甜嘴粉 的反， 米很惊，米也爽快地 ： "好，但你也不

要再叫我小!" "好，一言定。" 甜嘴粉 呱呱地叫着答。

Curious, Tommy moved closer to the cage. Sweet Pink looked as if she were in deep thought. She was a grey color with a dark red tail and grasped her perch strongly with her two feet. Tommy noticed each foot had two toes forward and two backward. There was a brass tag at the bottom of the cage that read (Psittcus erithaceus). Tommy wondered if Sweet Pink would talk again. "What is that word on your cage tag?" he asked.

"That's the type parrot I am," cawed Sweet Pink. "Did you know there are 315 different kinds of brightly colored birds?"

"Gee no," Tommy replied.

"I came from Africa and I am a particularly desirable type of parrot," Sweet Pink continued.

"WHY?" wide eyed Tommy exclaimed!

"Because I excel in imitating human speech," Sweet Pink answered.

汤米好奇的走近了笼子。甜嘴粉红看起来好像在沈思。它是一只灰色的鹦鹉，
有一条深红色的尾巴，两只脚强而有力地抓住树枝。
汤米注意到它的脚有两只脚趾向前和两只脚趾向后。笼子的底部有一个黄铜标记写着
(Psittcus erithaceus)。汤米心想不知道甜嘴粉红还愿意再说话。
"你笼子里的标记是什么意思?" 汤米问。

"我的鹦鹉类型," 甜嘴粉红呱呱地回答。

"你知道世界上有315种不同类型色彩缤纷的鸟吗?" "哇，不知道。," 汤米回答。

"我来自非洲并且是人们最喜欢的鹦鹉类型" 甜嘴粉红继续说。"为什么?"

汤米惊讶地睁大了双眼。"由于我擅长模仿人类讲话," 甜嘴粉红呱呱地回答。

"Oh," Tommy said, "I like talking to you, but let's do something fun. That will make us real friends."

"Good," Sweet Pink cawed. "We will fly over my African homeland."

"You can´t!" Tommy said. "There are tornadoes over Africa. I flew through them last night in my dream."

Sweet Pink's eyes twinkled and turned a soft wide black. "Trust me if we are to be friends," she said, "open the cage door and hurry outside."

"Wait a minute!" Tommy said. "Will you promise me that you'll get back in the cage when we're done playing?"

"I promise I will," Sweet Pink agreed.

"What now?" Tommy asked.

"I'm going to think big and you think small so you can ride on my back," Sweet Pink said.

"啊," 汤米说,"我喜欢跟你聊天，让我们一起做一些有趣的事。

那会使我们成为真正的朋友。" "好," 甜嘴粉红呱呱地回答。"我们将一起飞行，

飞去我在非洲的家园。" "你不能!" 汤米说。"非洲有龙卷风。我昨晚在梦中飞去过那里。

" 甜嘴粉红闪亮的眼睛渐渐变得柔和了： "相信我，如果我们是真正的朋友，

"它说, "打开笼子门，赶紧到外面去。"

Sweet Pink huffed and puffed and grew bigger and bigger.

Tommy scrunched up his face and fists and thought small, small, small. When he opened his eyes he couldn´t stop giggling. He was no bigger than a parakeet. His eyes opened wide when he looked at Sweet Pink. She was the same size as his silver jet!

In a flash, Sweet Pink and Tommy lifted off the houseboat just like the pigeons swarm up off the city streets. "Sweet Pink, it´s so quiet up here, and I can see and see and see everywhere!" Tommy said.

In no time they lost sight of the city as they flew over the Atlantic Ocean. Soon a dark image loomed upon the horizon.

"There's my homeland," Sweet Pink proudly boasted.

"等一等!"汤米说。"答应我,当我们飞行完之后,你会回到笼子来,

好吗?"我答应你,"甜嘴粉红同意。"我们怎么一起飞去?"汤米问。"用想象力 ─
我想象我会变得很大,你想象你会变得很小。那么,你就能你骑在我的背上。"
甜甜嘴粉红说。

甜嘴粉红一边吹气一边喷气,渐渐变得越来越大。汤米蜷缩起他的身子,
拼命的相像自己变小,小,小。当他张开了眼睛,他忍不住嘻嘻地笑起来。

他比长尾小鹦鹉还要小。当他看见甜嘴粉红,

它就像他的银色喷射机一样大!不一会儿,甜嘴粉红和汤米就升空离开了平底船屋了。

Tommy pointed. "And there's one of the tornadoes!"

"Yes, Tommy," Sweet Pink cawed, "here on the west coast of Africa we have tornadoes often in the summer."

"Just the way we have thunderstorms back in New York in the summer?" asked Tommy.

"Right," Sweet Pink answered.

Sweet Pink then changed her course and flew right next to the tornado.

"Can I bring it home?" Tommy pleaded. Sweet Pink nodded.

The tornado was gray. Tommy reached over and touched it. It moved so quick it tickled! It was air, it was like nothing. He put his arm around it and held the whirlwind tight.

"甜嘴粉红，天空是这样的宁静，我可以看见地面到处都是这样安静!" 汤米说。

渐渐的，城市隐没在脚下，他们飞到了大西洋上空。
很快一个黑暗的图像隐约地出现了在天际。"那儿是我的祖国，" 甜嘴粉红骄傲的说。

汤米指向黑影。"那是龙卷风!" "是, 汤米," 甜嘴粉红呱呱地回答，

"这里是非洲的西海岸。在夏天，我们经常有龙卷风。" "是不是像纽约，

夏天就有雷暴？" 汤米问。"对!" 甜嘴粉红答道。甜嘴粉红改变了它的飞行路线，

然后飞在龙卷风旁边。"我能带它回家吗?" 汤米恳求地问甜嘴粉红。甜嘴粉红点点头。

龙卷风是灰色的。汤米到达了龙卷风上面并伸手摸它。汤米想用手抓它，
但它移动得很快! 龙卷风是空气, 移动的空气。

"Hold on, we'll hurry back Tommy," Sweet Pink said, "Grandfather will worry if we're not there when he get's back."

Before Tommy knew it Sweet Pink was slowing down. Carefully braking with her wings, they gently slipped back into the houseboat.

Tommy's eyes were wide with mischief, "Where can I hide the tornado?" Tommy asked.

"Put it in the closet," Sweet Pink answered.

Grandfather soon came back. He saw Sweet Pink's eyes twinkling. He also saw Tommy's eyes shining. "Well, well," he said, "lets have a picnic lunch on the dock to celebrate this new friendship!"

"抓紧, 我们将赶回去, 汤米," 甜嘴粉红说。

"爷爷会担心我们如果他回来的时候我们不在家。" 汤米在不知不觉间,

甜嘴粉红已减慢了速度。 它小心地张开了翅膀, 轻轻地滑行到平地船屋放下汤米。

汤米睁大了淘气的双眼, "我能把龙卷风藏在那儿?" 汤米问。 "把它放进壁橱,"

甜嘴粉红回答。 爷爷很快回来了。他看见甜嘴粉红闪亮的眼睛。

他也看见汤米的眼睛充满光彩。"很好, 很好," 他说:
"让我们去船坞野餐庆祝这新友谊!"

When Grandfather went back out to the dock Tommy wanted to peek once more at his tornado. He opened the closet door, it was gone. He looked everywhere for it, but it wasn't there.

Where do you suppose it went?

当爷爷走去船坞时，汤米想再偷看一眼他的龙卷风。他打开了壁橱门，它已经离去。

他到处找它，但它已不在那里。"你猜它去了哪兒？"

THE
END

Joan Schaefer

Here I am in the Colorado Rocky Mountains. The sky is cobalt blue, mountain peaks snow white and slope-side, aspens show off as long stemmed beauties. A harvest moon, which reminds me so much of my Dad, looms large on the eastern horizon.

Blessings: it is summer of 2006. For me, a health mishap resulted in a prolonged recovery. The silver lining of this divine interlude was the generous gift of time, a time out from the rigors of everyday life. It was during this period I finished writing Sweet Pink. She has patiently waited to get off the ground, or I should say into the air...

Sweet Pink is on her way, I can't help but feel twinges of unpredictable joy. Steeped in tradition, story telling binds and spreads like a fragrance, from one generation to the next. I truly hope Sweet Pink is fun and a bit of a tease, whether you read it at school, on a subway, tucked in bed or gathered around a campfire with you and yours. Enjoy!

Practice Sheet
Characters

Actor   优人

Grandfather   王父

Actress   女伶

Mom   妈妈

Boy   僮

Tommy   托米

Bird   鸟

Sweet Pink   甜嘴粉红